The Trumpet has Sounded!

The Trumpet has Sounded!

John Masters

All rights reserved.

Copyright John Masters 2001

Cover Design by JGM 2001

01270 611212

www.thetrumpethassounded.com

Sound Books Publishing

ISBN 1 901044 08 4

Printed in Great Britain by Omnia Books.

This book is dedicated to
Sam, Ed, Jed,
and Charlie

Special appreciation to Carolyn Bounds
Texas, USA

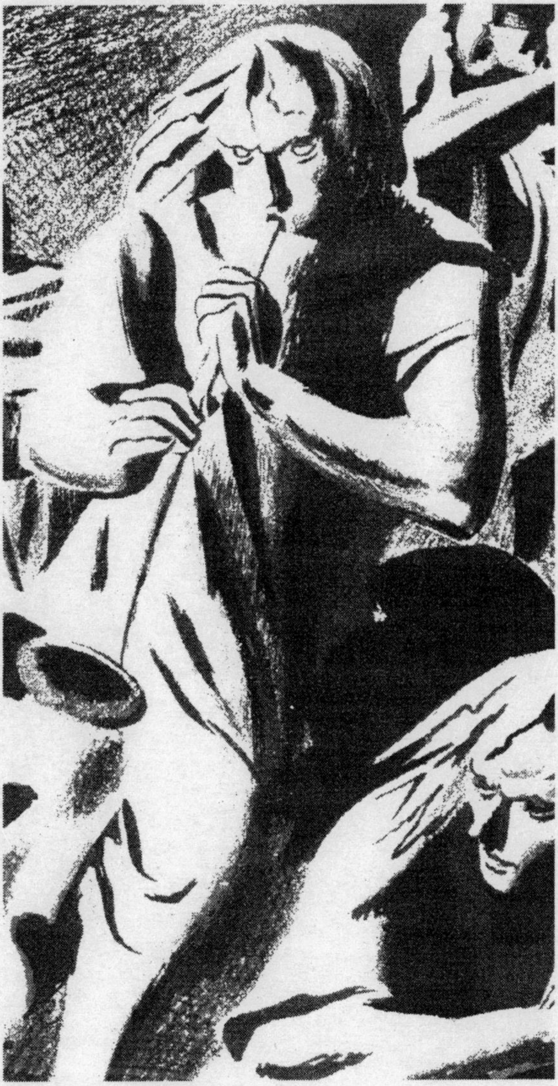

The Trumpet has Sounded!

Who can ever forget September 11th 2001? I received a phone-call around two o'clock in the afternoon, someone on the other end telling me to turn on the news. I, like everyone else was absolutely shocked.

Our world changed that day, and history was written indelibly in the lives of every human that walked on the planet.

Who could ever have predicted that such an outrageous and premeditated act of violence would be perpetrated in this the Western world?

I had to ask myself whether I was awake, or if this was just some bizarre nightmare. It was like watching a video, waiting for Bruce Willis to come racing along and save the day. But he did not. Neither did anyone else for that matter. Instead, the horror inflicted so deliberately by such inhuman infidels defied belief, yet remained embossed before our very eyes.

A trumpet sounded that day - a wake-up call to every person on the face of the earth. This was war, not just against the United States, but against democracy, against sensibility, and against all that is kind, gentle, or in the slightest bit good.

The world became less safe. We began to wonder who the person next door might be.

Within the space of a few hours the unknown terrorists had names and faces fitted to them by the FBI. They were no longer people we just passed in the street, but wretched and deadly opponents of all that is good and right. Masquerading as ordinary citizens, they harboured a revolting and obnoxious purpose. They were men with hidden agendas who walked among us as haters and despisers of our children, our parents, our friends and loved ones.

Maybe we had said, "good morning" to them,

or served them with groceries at the supermarket, or worked right alongside them in our daily duties. Not for a single moment did we ever imagine their utter disdain and disregard for humanity itself.

In the horror that ensued, my daughter telephoned me in tears. She has always loved New York, even though she has never been there. She told me how three years previously while at school, she had painted a picture of the very destruction that was now naked before our eyes.

In her mind she had seen those two towers all broken down, and for part of her school project she had painted that scene. Over in the right-hand corner she had drawn an eye with a tear running from it! She said, "I knew this was going to happen! I had already seen it!"

It was hard to come to terms with it over here in Great Britain. We have so many videos and films from America that it just seemed as unreal as they do. Even though a number of our own folk perished in the provocation, it was still hard to grasp the reality of it all.

I bought all the newspapers emblazoned with those horrendous pictures over the days following, and laid them out on the table and floor. I wanted to understand, and somehow get to grips with the shock, and hurt, and anger, and grief of the American people.

I guess that I, like so many others here, wanted to share in their suffering, their outrage and their mourning.

I did not want to be left out. I had to be, must be part of it all. I needed them, and they needed me, because we are one human race, and the power of this emotion is far too great for just one portion of humanity to bear it alone.

The pictures of those precious souls trapped on the upper levels above the flames and smoke, desperately seeking a way out, looking for a miracle that might bring them a speedy deliverance, brought tears to every eye.

The despair and fatefulness of those fragile beings who flung themselves to certain doom, choosing to die their own way, can never be fully explained or understood. We can but see a tragic hopelessness that defies any sort of comprehension.

And for those who perished in the flames, and those whose bodies were crushed and torn by the overwhelming collapse of those gigantic structures, the cry of the multitude rises to the highest heaven, and shall never be extinguished.

And as the days rolled on with page after page of dreadful stories emerging from the abyss of this human suffering, so the realisation of greater and more threatening scenarios was played out across our television screens.

A trumpet has sounded across the nations, a call to arms! An apocalyptic event has indeed changed our world!
A great and wretchedly evil deed has altered the course of life for tens of millions of ordinary folk.

Once more, religious fanaticism has displayed its cowardly face, sending its foolish slaves to do its ugly work, whilst its leaders hide in the dens and in the caves.

And wasn't it interesting to see the eagerness of some who shared that common goal, distancing themselves, just in case that wounded lion should rise again and take its violent revenge?

It was no less sinister to see the mocking and laughing faces of those who found it a matter of rejoicing.

Hitler sought his 'Master race', and these terrorists, no less, believe their cause the same, indeed upheld by God Himself.

But then history itself has seen a thousand similar causes that brought some untold misery to mums and dads and little children.

And all these passed away, and their grief remains forgotten like the early morning mist.

But I sense that this recent outrage was neither an end in itself, nor the climax of a restless and self-determined age.

The storm clouds gather - but not by chance of man, nor design of princes, but by event and consequence.

SEPTEMBER 11th 2001

Selfishness of Man's choice

I was thinking of those wretched men who through deceit and manipulation, climbed on board those air planes that morning. Looking around the cabins, they must have taken time to view the other passengers including the little children making their way excitedly to their seats.

Did anything in the appearance of those unthreatening faces disturb their thoughts at that time?

No, for their conscience was already desensitised through the anaesthesia of fanatical brainwashing.

Any decency or morality was benumbed by the selling of their souls to an enemy of all goodness and greatness.

As the branding iron burns the flesh, so these had yielded their hearts to the searing heat of self-centredness and self-determination.

Their goals were set in concrete, their plans wrought in iron, the stubbornness of their wills inflexible and unwavering.

Driven by what they believed to be right in their own eyes, they had surrendered themselves to their own delusions. It did not matter who was on board that plane. It could have been full, or it could have been empty. It mattered not one bit either way.

They were masters of their own destiny, and in their fierce determination to do whatever they chose to do, they did not care who got in the way or who got hurt.

This was not a sudden decision taken on the spur of the moment. This was no momentary lapse of common-sense or responsibility. These men had sold themselves to do evil with both hands.

At any time after they had taken their seats they could have changed their minds and sought to mend their ways, but alas, their souls were quite dead.

The provoking voice of conscience, that must surely have been there at one time, had been defied for too long. Chasing after a wicked intention robbed them of their morals. The unwholesome company that they kept poisoned their rationale, intoxicating their desires for evil

As they say, "Bad company spoils good manners."

They believed a lie.

They thought that they were right. They truly believed they were doing the correct thing, that would in the end win them some sort of favour with God.

They even had the nerve to believe that God would reward them for such outrageous acts, and grant them grace, and let them into His heaven!

It occurred to me that here was a picture of the whole of our modern society. We all seek our own cause and comfort. We plan our own futures and direction. We set our hearts on the things that we most want in life, and do all we can to acquire and achieve those ends. Sometimes the voice of reason comes along and challenges us to a duel, but we have mastered the sword of selfishness, and have learned how to wield it to our own satisfaction!

No one can move us from our own obstinate desire.
We do it as individuals, and we do it as nations.
And in pursuing our own aims and goals, we board whichever plane will take us closest to our presumed destinies.
We may feel that we have some sort of right to get on board and travel to these presupposed locations. In our greed and

ambition though, we are not content to be led by another, but have to take control ourselves of the plan.

So, just like those terrorists, we abuse the privilege of trust, and despise authority by attempting to take over where we have no right to be.

They broke into the flight deck and defied the authority that was placed there. They commandeered that position, and in effect said,

"We will do it our way!"

In our lives we are all on board some flight or other, heading to our predetermined finale. Perhaps we should spare a thought for all those who travel with us. What about our own family and loved ones? Do we truly care enough to preserve and protect them from all danger, even though it may spoil our plans to do so?

Who knows how many travel on the same craft with us? All of our lives are intricately interwoven with so many others. The fact that we even exist has a relevance to dozens, hundreds, perhaps thousands of other people, even people we do not know yet.

Choices are important. Each choice that we make in life will undoubtedly have an impact on so many others around us.
For instance, suppose I decide to go out drinking, and end up driving my vehicle back home under the influence of alcohol. I have chosen to do what I wanted, to drown my sorrows in the bottle, or just to live it up for a few hours.

So, having surrendered my common-sense to another master, I end up having a terrible accident along the road. Maybe I end up killing someone, or crippling another, as well as myself. Just think of the countless interactions involved in such a tragedy - mums, dads, brothers, sisters, children, friends, all bereaved of someone they were personally involved with.

Think of all the sadness, loneliness, and emptiness of houses and lives where only photographs remain. Think of the comments as in years to come relatives might say, "Oh, I wish you could have met him; he was such a kind person, and he was so gifted."

But my choice to live my life how I pleased ended up shaping and changing the destiny of so many others as well as my own.

It would be good to question ourselves from

time to time, and examine our own ways. Where are we going? What effect are we having on those who travel this journey with us?

Somebody once asked me what I would ask for if I was granted just one wish in life. I thought about that for a few moments. There is so much to consider.
I replied, "If I could have one thing, it would be that I might be right!"
They answered me, and said, "But you are right about many things. What do you mean?"
I said, "You misunderstand me. When I say I want to be right, I mean that I want to be right in what I do with my life. I want to be right when I get up in the morning; I want to be right in the way I live through the day; and I want to be right when I come to the end of my

time in this world, because there is no greater thing than to leave this place knowing that my heart is right."

That word 'right' has everything to do with being 'righteous'.

The great problem with the human race is that we are all wrong, and the only true cure for this desperate generation is to be right. I shall address this a little further on in these pages.

When I choose to live my life on my terms, the chances are that I will bring great hurt and damage to many other innocents. I may be quite oblivious to the grief that I am causing simply because I can see no further than the end of my own greedy nose.

The story of Jonah and the whale (great fish,

for those who are fussy!) is quite pertinent in this scenario. He chose to go his own way even though he had been instructed to do what was right.

He found a ship and went down into the hold to run away from the truth, and there he went to sleep.

The story goes that a great storm was sent from God because of his disobedience, and the captain of the ship and all his mates were fighting for their lives as the ship began to fill with water. They subsequently lost everything that they had because it became necessary to throw it all overboard.

In their desperation they searched the boat and discovered this fellow sleeping down below.

They were astonished that he was not even aware of the awful plight that they were in.

They said, "How can you sleep at a time like this?"

What a frightful condition to be in: to go through life oblivious to the terror and affliction our rebellion brings on others.

The truth hit him in the face, and he had to acknowledge that he was the cause of all their distress. He told them to throw him out of the ship, and despite all their efforts to try and bring that vessel under control, they were obliged to do that very thing.

As soon as he was gone, the wind stopped, the waves settled, and the sky cleared.

I thought about the third plane, and the stories that emerged of the heroic efforts of a few trapped in that human missile. Their valiant decisions that day may well have saved thousands of more lives on the ground.

Again, the decisions we all make have the most profound consequences on the lives of so many others. We may never know in this world who we may or may not have affected.

Selfishness takes no thought for anyone else, but only seeks to please itself.

At any point or moment in time those hijackers could have changed their minds, stopped what they were doing, and altered their course. Any one of them could have turned around.

Instead of being the lethal and destructive influence that they were, they could have been the means of saving thousands of lives. We all have choices.

It is easy to place the blame on someone else, or even on God or the devil. "I couldn't help myself!" is a feeble and unwarranted excuse.

To own up and be honest with ourselves is the beginning of our own help. We all make decisions, good and bad. We are all given the chance to turn around.

This trumpet that has sounded calls us to wake up to the truth. It demands that we get off this train of endless madness and reflect on the real issues of life.

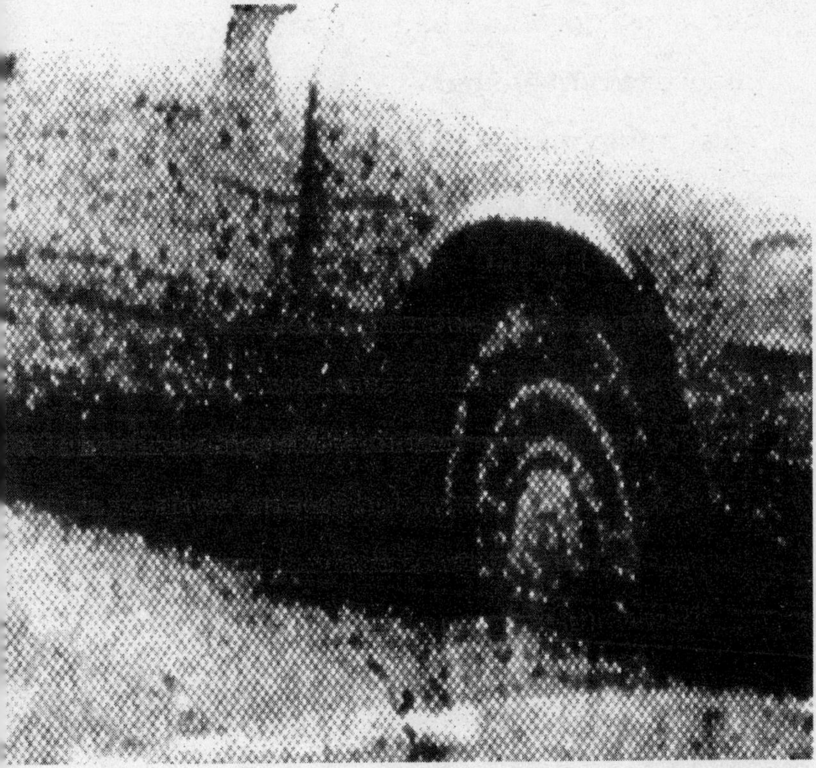

Life is a Vapour

Looking at the pictures of all those cars around the streets where the twin towers once stood, one could not help but wonder where each of their owners were. Some undoubtedly had escaped the horror, whilst others would never come back to collect their possessions.
It brings you to your senses as you see such a pitiful sight.

People's dreams, young men's pride, young women's achievements all lying in the dust of life.

The executive and the manager, along with the cleaner and the waitress, all separated forever from what they had spent hours working for.

It makes you wonder what life is all about, doesn't it?

We spend our days labouring for things that have no lasting substance. It sort of brings everything into context.

Somebody once said, "What is your life? - even a vapour." Like the steam from a kettle, it appears for a while, and then vanishes away.

As soon as we are able, we set out to plan our lives and lifestyle, deciding which way we will go to achieve the dreams that we have.

We plot our course and hope that fate and 'luck' will serve us well.

We do not know the number of our days, but live our lives as though they will go on forever. That's why the terminating of so many beautiful lives has shocked us all so very much.

Life suddenly seems so fragile and delicate.

A great man once likened our lives to pitiful beings whose substance is suspended by a fine silver thread. No one knows when that thread might break.

Suppose a man should have a dream, and build himself some great buildings, and deposit all of his wealth and treasure in them. Suppose that he should pat himself on the back, and stand admiringly at all that his hand has achieved. Hear him say, "My, you have done well for yourself; look at what you have made; that is what you call success!" Supposing he should satisfy himself and say, "You can take it easy now, sit back and enjoy the rest of your life; you have earned it, you deserve it, go on, take it easy!"

And what if there comes the trumpet call that very night, and says, "Tonight your soul is required, today you must leave this world"?
What value is there to him in all that he has worked for and acquired throughout his days?
Can any of it be taken where he is going?
Will any of his treasure purchase any good in the future life?
Naked he came into this world, and naked he shall depart.
If we only have treasure in this world we are a most miserable bunch. If there is no future

life, then what on earth is the point in us being here now?

When the trumpet sounded in America, it was a call to all people everywhere to consider the substance of life, and the demands of eternity.

Oh yes, the trumpet has sounded, and only fools would ignore it.

A trumpet will sound for everyone of us someday, rich, poor, educated, illiterate. None of us can escape it, and for thousands this very day, even this hour, it is already sounding. Just in the last twenty four hours multitudes have left this world and passed into eternity, quite unprepared.

The trumpet has sounded, and yet there is a greater and more awesome trumpet than this, waiting its turn to summon the world, and stand us all to attention.

E.M.

Why???

The big question that rages silently in the hearts of millions around the world. "Why did it happen? Why did God allow it? Why did they all die so terribly?"

This is the question that finds no place of reconciliation in the minds of so many who lost someone special that morning.

Some of these questions we can never know the answer to.

When my father died I asked God, perhaps in some measure demanded God, "Why?" "It doesn't make sense. Its not fair! Its not right."

I heard some callous and despicable remarks that suggested these people in America *deserved* to die for some reason or another! Certainly in the mind of those 'fundamentalists' they were worthy of death, no matter how horrific that end.

There is a story related in the Bible, almost like two recent headliners from the local press. Some men came to Jesus and said, "Look at this wicked act of terrorism: Pilate has butchered and murdered some of the religious folk during their holy sacrifices, and mixed their blood with the blood of the animals!"

The question silently posed was, "Why?"

The answer was certainly not what they were expecting. I guess they thought he would show His anger and outrage at this attack, but He did not.

He said, "Do you think that those who died were perhaps more bad than other folk, and that is why they perished in such a vile manner?

No! and I tell you that unless you yourselves turn back to God and get right with Him, you also will perish!"

And if that was not enough, He went on to tell of another recent story where a tower-block had fallen on a number of men, killing them outright.

He said again, "Do you think that these men died because they were worse sinners than other people?

Let Me assure you that unless you turn back to God, you also will perish!"

It is quite amazing to see how 'on target' the Bible is at times like these.

The unspoken question came back with a loaded challenge.

So the question that lies heavy in the air is answered with the same challenge to each and every one of us.

The trumpet has sounded, and brought us all to attention.

This clarion call must not be ignored. "Consider your ways!" it cries, "and turn, even turn with all your heart, before a worse thing comes upon you."

Why did God see fit to allow this?

Maybe we should be asking, "What is God saying to us *through* all this?"

The trouble is that we only seem to want His advice and help when we have got ourselves into a mess.

The stage is being set right now for the fulfilment of biblical prophecy. When you read certain parts of the Bible, it is like reading tomorrow's newspapers.

A great battle is going to be waged in the Middle East, according to the Bible. All the nations round about Israel will come against her to destroy her. Even Russia will come and fight against her.

This last conflict will be known as 'Armageddon' ("the mount of Megiddo"). Revelation tells us that this final war will be defined as 'the great day of God Almighty'.

At the moment all eyes should be on Israel, because according to the Bible, she is the timepiece of this world. So much of this present conflict is over Israel and those who support her.

We are also told that when the armies surround her to destroy her, at the very moment she seems to be utterly vanquished, God Himself will step into the whole situation and call down fire from heaven upon her enemies.

"I will gather all nations against Jerusalem to battle; and the city shall be taken. Then shall the Lord God go forth, and fight against those nations. And His feet shall stand on the mount of Olives......

And this shall be the plague with which the Lord God shall smite all the people that have fought against Jerusalem; Their flesh shall consume away while they stand upon their feet, and their eyes shall consume away in their holes, and their tongue shall consume away within their mouths."

"And the kings (rulers) of the earth, and the great men, and the rich men, and the chief captains, and the mighty men, and the [conscripts and volunteers] hid themselves in the dens and in the rocks of the mountains; And said to the mountains and rocks, "fall on us, and hide us from the face of Him who sits on the throne...... for the great day of His wrath is come; and who shall be able to stand?"

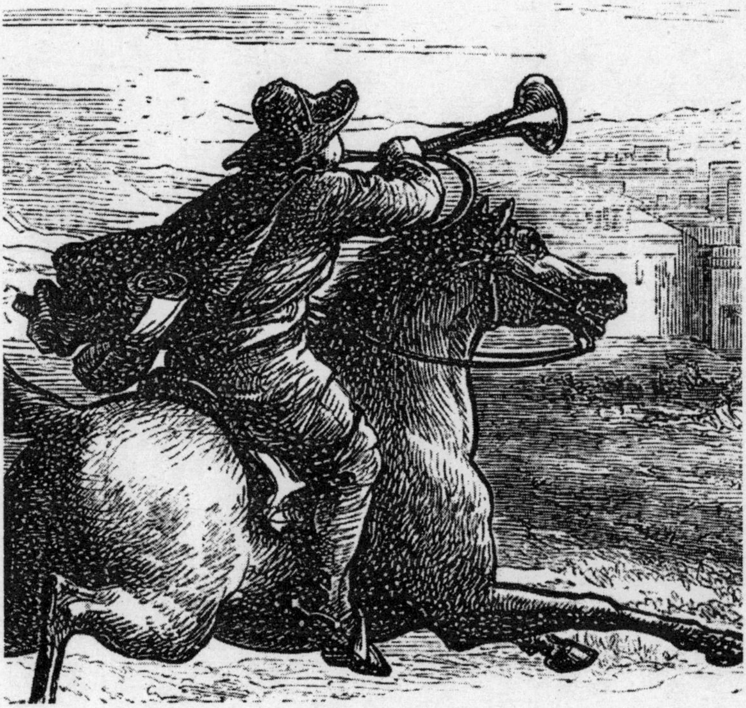

The Second Horseman

When they shall say, "Peace, peace", then watch out for sudden destruction!

The trumpet has sounded, but what trumpet, and who for?

What happened on September 11th 2001 was not just an act of terrorism, but the sounding of a distinct note heralding a new age, a new dispensation. Our anticipated utopia, our hopes of peace and tranquillity quickly evaporated by the time the second plane had impacted those great symbols of success and prowess.

Until then most of us thought that we had 'got away with it', i.e. having to go through the possibilities of a world at war, or the catastrophe of multitudes dying through the letting off of a nuclear device.

There have been several near-misses over the last fifty years, but we have been very grateful that somehow or other we managed to avoid such calamities.

A great deal of the film industry has centred on nightmarish possibilities, with one of our great heroes rallying the troops, and saving the day.

Interestingly, many of these scenarios depict New York as being the epicentre for the looming disaster or threat. We have been conditioned into expecting the only acceptable outcome - that just in the nick of time, our 'saviour', the star of the film, will, against all the odds, deliver the final punch, and KO the problem.

No matter how impossible or improbable the answer, we are all delighted to see the world righted once more, and its citizens living in peace and harmony.

We have been nicely lulled into a sense of false security, but now powerfully awakened to the reality of a world filled with violence and violent people.

This is not a film, this is not a dream, this is as real as it gets!

The book of Revelation speaks of four horsemen riding out in the closing chapters of this world. Each one carries a particular emblem. I was most interested to read of the second horseman, and what it was that he carried.

"And there went out another horse that was red: and power was given to him that sat thereon to take peace from the earth, and that they should kill one another: and there was given unto him a great sword."

One of our daily newspapers over here had for its front-page headline on September 12th, "APOCALYPSE", with a picture of Manhattan looking like a scene from 'Independence Day'.
The book of Revelation is called the Apocalypse because it is the uncovering of the future and final days of this world. It was written nearly two thousand years ago, but

rings so loud and clearly in this present age. It has an acute relevance to it.

I wondered if there is some sort of parallel to the significance of this second horse and its rider. Perhaps that rider has now begun his apocalyptic ride throughout the earth.
He is given power to take peace from the earth.
In one mind-shattering blow, that has already happened, and who knows where all this is leading now? The fragile peace that we did have was only skin-deep anyway, but now it is being stretched to breaking point across the nations.
Proud and pompous words have been spoken by leaders throughout the world, and their threats have been replied to with retaliations. Men in high office have arrogantly vaunted

their position as though they were above it all.

God is not mocked, not even by those who strut around in their pomp and show.

If ever there was a time to call the nation to prayer, it must be now. If ever there was a time to be humble and put away wickedness from our lives, it must be now.

If ever there was a right time to come off our high horses and ask God for wisdom, this is that time.

The lofty looks shall be brought down. It is the humble person who walks with God.

The day of the Lord will come upon every one who is proud and haughty, and they shall be brought down.

Coming back to this second horse....

A great sword is given to this heavenly rider, and you can almost hear the cry as he goes out, "The sound of battle is in the land!"

This appears to indicate the rising up of nation against nation, and the deadly disease of war and hatred being spread right around the globe.

"For nation will rise against nation, and kingdom against kingdom; there shall be famines, and epidemics, and earthquakes, in different places.

All these are the beginnings of sorrows."

At the moment it is not hard to see just how easily this could escalate. A great cloud of darkness seems to have arisen seeking to engulf the whole of the planet in self-destruction.

"The sound of battle is in the land; the time is fulfilled, and the kingdom of God is at hand: repent (turn around) and believe the gospel."

I was in a meeting in Birmingham two days before the strike on New York. Before the programme commenced I had this strange sense of foreboding, and shared with the people gathered that I believed a dark cloud was coming filled with threatening and trouble.

Somebody near me said, "It is already here!" I replied, "Not this one! This one is far worse than anything else we have seen so far."

In less than forty-eight hours that cloud had stretched its dark and ominous shadow across the heart of America.

The Bible talks about a night that is coming in which no one can work. It will be such an evil and horrific period that we had better make sure we know whose side we are on.

It will not be a choice between this country or that country, or between East and West. It will not be a choice between this army or that one, but it will be a decision about who we choose to serve in our lives, and whether we stand on the rock, or run with the crowd.

The choice, as ever, will be the choice between good and evil, between what is right and what is wrong. The choice for each one of us will be that of serving God, or that of siding with the devil.

At times like these there will always be an upsurge in the antics of the cults, especially those like the Jehovah's Witnesses. The frustrating thing about this is that they see the possibility of fitting their own beliefs into the Bible's prophecies. Don't be fooled. Religion never made anyone free.

Religion is in itself a form of slavery. Keeping sets of rules, and having to conform to lists of do's and don'ts does not give you liberty, but rather puts you under burdens that wear you down and grind your soul. Jesus Christ said, "You shall know the truth, and the truth shall make you free!"

He also said, "I have come that you might have life, and have it in all its abundance!" On another occasion He said that He was the way, the truth, and the life, and that whoever comes to Him will not walk in darkness or deception.

The only true course in the days ahead is to put our trust in the Rock, - Jesus the Son of God.

How do I do that?

By believing in Him with all of my heart. By turning from my sin and my unbelief, and by receiving Jesus Christ into my life right here, right now.

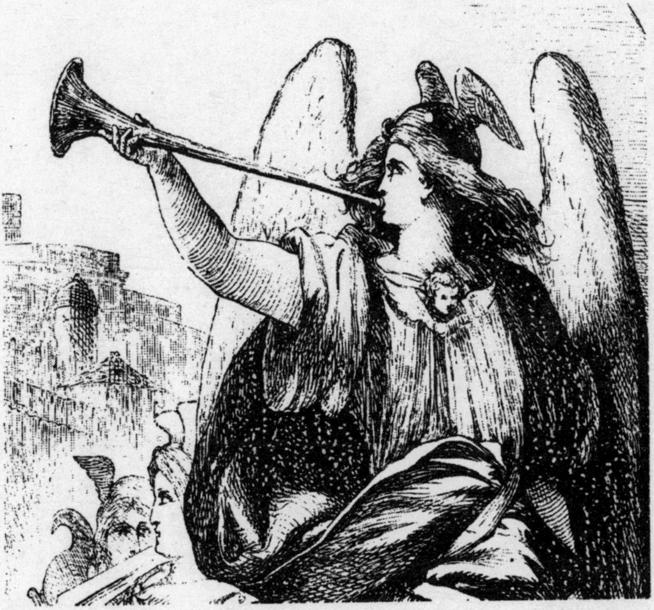

Seven Trumpets Sound

So, have you ever wondered what the future holds?
I suppose that everyone of us has thought about it from time to time, but on the whole we prefer to ignore it and live our lives as they come day by day.
"Eat, drink, and be merry, for tomorrow we die! - We'll worry about it when it happens!"

Yet thousands visit fortune tellers and look into crystal balls to see what is in store for them. There is a natural curiosity in all of us that wants to enquire into the forbidden zone. However, the secret things belong to God, but the things that He has revealed are ours to consider.

So while people wonder what will happen in the coming days, there is a whole big and astonishing revelation of the future already in print. It talks quite specifically of world-wide events and the closing chapters of this age.

Want to know more?

It speaks of seven angels with seven trumpets. On the sounding of each trumpet a different world-changing event begins to manifest itself.

The first trumpet blasts, and 'hail and fire mingled with blood is cast to the earth; a third of all trees are burnt up, and all green grass is destroyed.'

This trumpet heralds massive destruction and death on a world-wide scale.

I wonder what proportion of trees have been destroyed over recent years, or for that matter how much of the grass has been lost?

But what of the first part - 'hail and fire mingled with blood'?

The second trumpet sounds, and a great mountain burning with fire is cast into the sea, and a third part of the seas are poisoned, and a third part of the creatures in the sea die. Furthermore, a third of all the shipping is destroyed.

The third trumpet sounds, and a great burning star falls from heaven as bright as a great lamp. It falls onto a third of the fresh water sources, the rivers and the springs. It poisons the waters, and many die from the pollution.

You may not want to know what the other four trumpets foretell, but you can check them out in the Bible if you are at all interested.

As these things begin to happen these passages will start to make a great deal of sense.

Revelation chapter eight reveals even more frightening and awesome details of things that are coming to this world.

Maybe you think that these things cannot be true.

A couple of years ago around Christmas, my eldest son Samuel was having a bit of a hard day, and decided to take it out on me! He said, "This 'God-thing', - you know, my friends say it can't possibly be true!"

He was just trying to get at me and see if I would take the bait!

I said to him, "Sam, supposing that I told you that I have buried £8,000 in the garden at the back of the house, - would you believe me?"

He replied, "Of course not!"

I said, "But what if I really have? Just because you do not believe me does not alter the fact that there is a load of cash hidden in the soil."

He said that I would never do such a crazy thing, shrugged his shoulders and walked off.

Some weeks later, around the second week in January, he was 'grounded' by his mother for some misdemeanour or other. He came to me about eight o'clock at night begging me to lift his confinement to the house. I told him that he would have to do his time, and could go out the following evening. Well, he just kept on at me, trying to get me to change my mind!

I had a thought. I said, "Do you remember when I mentioned about burying £8,000 in the ground?"

He said, "Yes, and I told all my friends at school about that. They said that not even my dad would be that mad, to bury so much money in the flower-bed!"

I offered him a deal. I said, "If I can prove to you that the money is in the garden, would you be willing to stop whining and do your discipline, and stay in?" He said, "Yes! but I know you are only kidding, so let me go out."

I suggested that he get the shovel from the garden shed and dig a hole somewhere.

He thought that he saw through a rather

cleverly designed plan to get him to dig the whole garden, and utterly refused.

As I went out to get the spade I could hear him laughing away indoors, but he looked out of the window watching me as I dug a hole of around three feet deep.

I came across a piece of plastic pipe, and brushing the dirt off, brought it into the house. He just laughed again.

As I removed the tape that was securing each end of that 4" diameter tube, he sniggered. I reached inside and pulled out a bag. Tossing it over to him, I suggested that he take a look inside. I think that his eyes nearly popped out of his head!

"Count it!" I said, " I believe that you will find eight, that is eight thousand pounds in there." He counted it.

I said, "See! I told you, even if you do not believe it, it makes no difference to the truth. The truth will always be the truth."

I anticipated a lot of very eager young gardeners coming round for a job in the next few weeks!

So, even if you do not believe what the Bible says, if it is the truth, then it is going to happen anyway.

Your unbelief cannot change the truth. However, your 'not-believing' can positively confirm your ultimate destiny.

Your Ultimate Destiny.

Can we really know our ultimate destiny? And if we know it, is it possible to change it?

Did you ever watch Spielberg's film, 'Schindler's List'? If you remember, Schindler drew up a list of Jews who were condemned to certain death under the Nazi regime during World War 2. By taking them on as employees in his factory, he gave them a way out of what proved to be mass genocide on proportions that are quite unimaginable. This list became their salvation and their passport to a future that would not exist for them otherwise.

By his heroic and loving intervention he made a way for them to escape, and changed their destinies in this world.

The destiny of mankind is recorded. Our individual destinies are also recorded. Governments keep records of every birth, and every death that occurs. They also keep records of our health, our marital status, our tax payments, our ability to drive, our criminal behaviour, and so on.

God also keeps records. He has a record of every person who ever lived and lives. He has a record of our lives, of every word that we have spoken, every deed that we have done, every thought that has entered our minds.

He has a record of every secret hidden in our lives!

He also has a record of everyone's eternal destiny.

We are all born at a specific time, and we are all going to die one day. None of us knows quite when that is, but the fact is that everyone on this planet will die.

The Bible says that, 'after death there is judgement.'

Death is not the end.

There is judgement seen in this world, but there is a greater judgement to come after this life is over and done.

The book of the Revelation (the last book in the Bible) tells us that everyone of us, both great and small, both rich and poor, shall stand before God to give account of our lives.

Look at what it says:

"And I saw a great white throne, and Him that sat on it, from whose face heaven and earth fled away;

and I saw the dead, small and great, stand before God; and the books were opened: and another book was opened, which is the book of life: and the dead were judged out of those things which were written in the books.

And the sea gave up the dead which were in it; and death and the grave delivered up the dead which were in them:

they were judged every one according to their works.

And death and the grave were cast into the Lake of Fire. This is the second death.

And whoever was not found written in the Book of Life was also cast into the Lake of Fire."

This passage tells of a frightening day when everyone is summoned to appear before a holy God. This has nothing to with the religion you adhere to. Neither does it have anything to do with the denomination or church that you may or may not attend. This is not a day of reckoning for those with some sort of faith, but is the dividing line where all of our destinies will be meted out.

This truly is the line of separation.

We see a number of books being opened in heaven, and then reference to 'another book' being opened. This book has a unique title. It is called 'the Book of Life.'

We quickly discover that anyone and everyone whose name does not appear in this Book of Life has an unspeakable and dreadful destiny awaiting them. According to the Bible, this is the future of those who reject

God and deny His Son as being the Saviour of the world.

In actual fact, the Bible speaks of this place on numerous occasions, and Jesus referred to it time and time again. It is called 'hell'.

There are some modernist preachers and ministers who do not believe this, probably because they don't want to loose their jobs. If they upset their congregations by talking about it, then the people will leave and go elsewhere! (Don't be tricked into believing that everyone who goes to church will also go to heaven.)

However, I would sooner believe the Bible (after all, it is God's own message to us), than put my faith in a man, no matter how clever he may seem.

If trouble is coming our way, then we need to know about it so that we can find a way to avoid it if possible. I would rather know the truth about the future, than discover it too late to do anything about it.

If any of the people on those planes that morning in September had been told the truth about their destination, there is not one of them who would not have turned around, left the aircraft, and ran the other way.

If any of those thousands of office workers and executives had had the slightest insight into the horror that was already heading their way in those early hours, they would have fled the buildings with all their might.

I suppose though, that there would always have been those who said, "I don't believe it. That could never happen. God would never allow that to happen!"

But for all those who had no warning whatsoever, it was too late. It was too late *before* the planes impacted and exploded because no message of advice had been sent either from the perpetrators of the crime, or the intelligence agencies who should have had some foreknowledge of the event.

Great blame is being laid at the doors of the FBI and CIA and other agencies, because it is their job to watch out for their people and their country.

They are the trumpet-blowers.

They must be on the lookout for all threats and dangers, and be ready to waken the people to the trumpet's blast.

That is why this book is called 'The Trumpet has Sounded!'

It is my job, along with millions of other Christians, to sound a warning to the peoples of this world, "Prepare to meet your God!"

None of us can escape meeting God. Better to meet Him in this life, and make peace with Him now, than to have to stand before Him on that great and terrible day of judgement.

My prayer is that good will come out of evil. If this shocking catastrophe serves to warn America, Great Britain, and the rest of this world of the fragility of our lives, and the impending judgements of God, then let us take note. It may well be that thousands will take advantage of God's mercy, and grace, and forgiveness that He offers at this time.

The devil's job is to hide the truth from you, blind your mind, so that you cannot believe the gospel (God's message of good news to us).

The Bible tells us that God so loves this world, that He gave his only begotten Son

(Jesus), that *whoever* believes on Him shall not perish, but have everlasting life!

While there is breath in your body, and life in your blood, there is hope that you can find a different destiny. But once you have departed this life, that chance has been and gone.

That is why this book is important. It may be your last chance to hear from God, believe in Jesus Christ, and find forgiveness and salvation.

The Bible says there is salvation (deliverance) in no other name but the name of Jesus.

Ignore the battle-cry if you wish, bury your head in the sand like the ostrich, but be certain that you have now been given fair warning, and have absolutely no excuse for not turning to God and repenting of your sin.

If you choose to ignore or deny this message, then you do indeed refuse the only possible way out.

That is what the Bible says. 'How shall we escape the things to come if we make light of the things put before us?'

"For God has appointed a day in which He will judge the world in righteousness..."

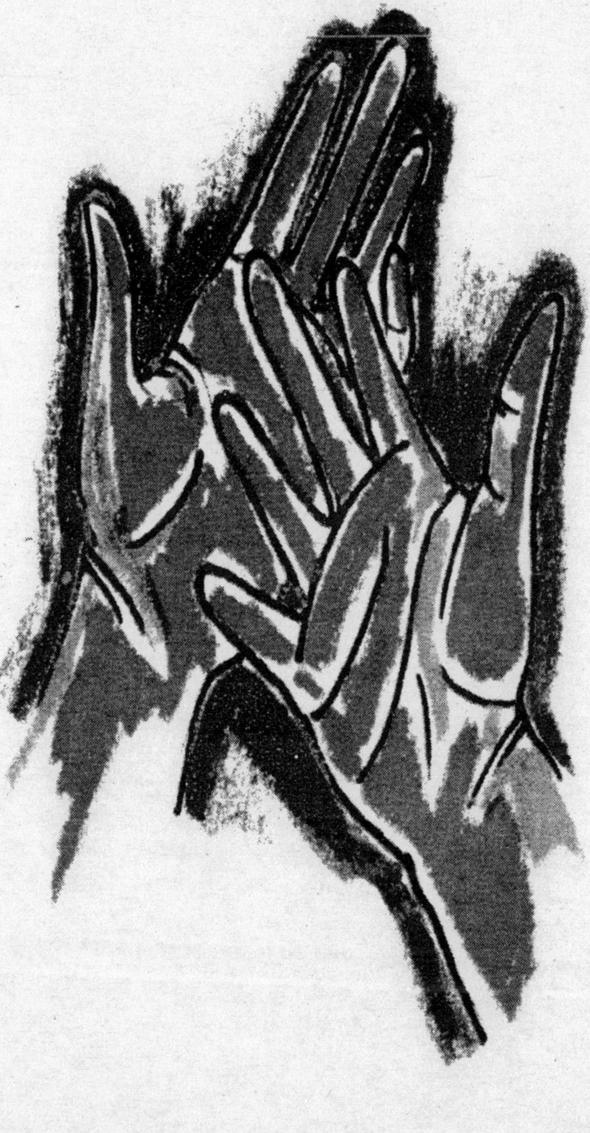

What exactly is this 'Book of Life' and how do I get my name into it?

The Bible makes it profoundly clear that the only people who go to heaven and escape their ultimate destiny are those whose names are written in this book that God has.
Let us make no mistake. Hell was prepared by God for the devil and all the angelic beings that follow him - not for man.

If however man chooses to live a life without God as his centre, then he must also accept a fate without God or His goodness.

That fate is the same as that which is afforded the devil. If you choose to follow his deceptions, then you choose also to share his destiny.

But God, who is rich in mercy and goodness, has made a way for us fallen creatures to escape the consequence of our sin.

The Bible says that the wages of sin is death, - that is not just physical death (which proves the case that we are all sinners, for indeed we all die), but also spiritual death.

The gift of God is eternal life.

This spiritual death is not some form of annihilation where we cease to exist. In fact, the Bible teaches that man has both a body, a soul, and a spirit. Physical death is not the end.

What happens when we die?

It is a question that many would love to know, but no one has ever come back to tell us. Do we just go to sleep and not exist anymore, or is there something else out there?
In fact, Jesus did come back from the dead, and He spoke about the world beyond this world.
It is nothing to do with whether you have done enough good things to go to heaven, or bad things and deserve to go to hell.
Going to church does not guarantee any sort of peace or reconciliation with God. "Unless you repent you shall perish," is what He said.

To 'repent' means to 'turn around and face God', to 'about turn' from where I am and where I'm headed. It requires that I believe what God says about my sin, about His Son, and about His offer of forgiveness.

To repent means that I am willing to leave my old ways, and surrender my life to God.

We need to be sure that our name is written in the Book of Life before we go any further. If it is not, then now is the time to do something about it.

Jesus died on the cross for sinners and for their sin. All who believe on Him are forgiven and acquitted. Their names get written in that book the moment they receive Jesus Christ into their hearts by faith.

The blood that Jesus shed on the cross is the only thing in the whole of the universe that can wash away my sin - not my good works, not me 'turning over a new leaf', not me joining some religious order. None of this can save me.

"The blood of Jesus Christ God's Son cleanses us from all sin." And unless I believe that, I have no hope of having my name in the book that guarantees my future.

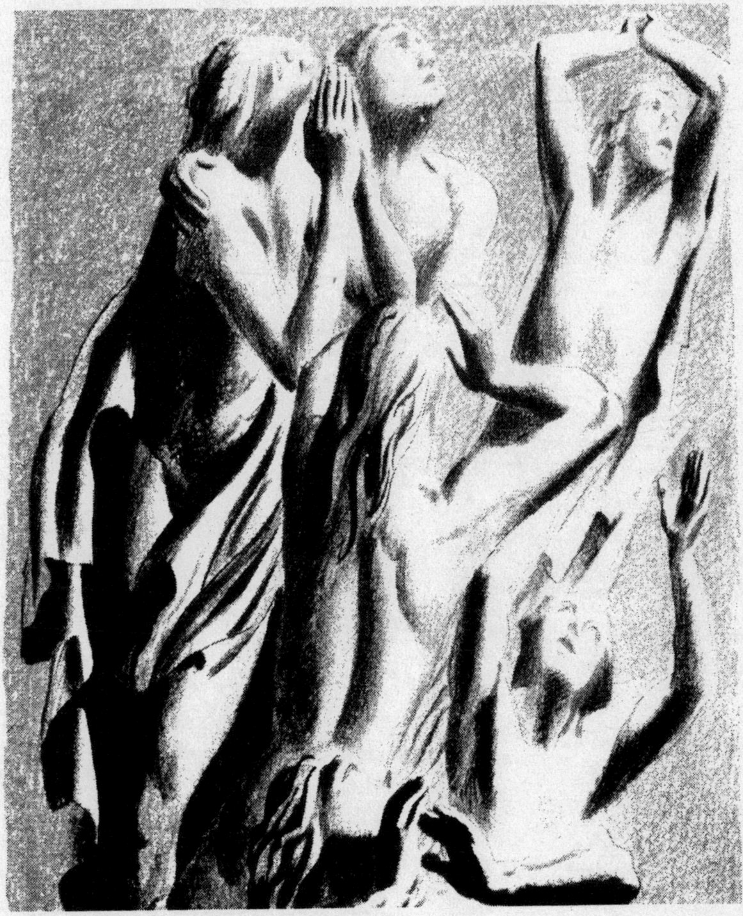

Destiny of a Blackbird

I was out taking a walk early one morning this year gathering my thoughts before the day began.
As I came back down the road, I saw what looked like a dead blackbird lying in the gutter. It would appear that it had been struck down by a vehicle. Although it still

seemed to be alive, I figured that before very long it would either be run over again, or just die from its injuries.

I walked on, thinking, "Well, there's nothing that I can do about it; I'm not a bird doctor, and anyway it looks like it is destined to die so long as it sits there on the tarmac."

I began to think how sad it was that the birds and animals were so helpless. We the human race can call on assistance to fix us up and help us when we are injured. We have hospitals, and nurses, and ambulances. We have medicines, and bandages, and a host of technology, to come to our rescue and relief. These poor creatures have nothing.

I turned round and went back up the road to where this bird had fallen. I looked at it, and thought that if I reached down and picked it up, it would probably peck me and scratch my hand.

Nevertheless, I took it in my hands and nestled it under my coat.

On arriving home my children wanted to see what I had found. They were quite excited when I showed them, and asked whether it would live.

I said that I did not know, but if we brought it into the warm and left it some water and bread, maybe it would recover.

Well, I brought it into the study, and placed it on the floor.

Some time later we discovered that it had managed to fly up onto the curtain rail where it sat quite still for the next eight hours. Even when we walked right up to it, it would not move, except to turn its head.

That evening we had a training course in the study for over three hours. Still the bird did not move, except occasionally to turn its head and look at us.

The next morning I went into the room and found the bird flying around. I left it there with some fresh bread for a few more hours.

In the afternoon I opened the window, and watched in amazement as it flew straight out and disappeared into the branches of a tall tree some 300 yards away.

Some young Muslim graduates once asked me why God, being so big and so great, should need to make His Son a man in order to save our lives. "If God is so huge, why would He bother to make Himself so small to come and save us?"

They told me that they believed in God, and in Jesus, but could not understand why the

Bible teaches that God disguised Himself as a man to come and rescue us.

I asked them whether they had ever seen an anthill. They said, "Yes, of course."

I said, "Supposing that that anthill got all trodden on, and broken down, and all those little ants got damaged and hurt. Could you get inside that house of theirs, and fix up their poor little bodies? Could you put together the bits and pieces of their lives?"

They replied, "No, of course not!"

I said, "Why not?"

They said, "Because we're too big!"

I said, "Exactly! And God was far too big to reach down and fix us all up after our lives had been destroyed and hurt through sin, so He stepped down into this world of frail humanity - as a man - in the weakness of manhood, to save us the only way that we could be saved."

They said, "Wow!"

The blackbird's destiny was changed when I came along the road. It needed someone else to help it, or the next truck that came along would certainly have finished it off.
It accepted my intervention and care, and by being still, and safe, it was made whole again.
I don't know for sure whether it was the same blackbird or not, but one that looked very similar with a damaged wing, came and sat in a tree near my window every morning for months afterwards. It would sing constantly so long as it was there, and even when I walked outside, it would not fly away.

I could walk right up to the branches where it was perched, and it showed no fear.

What you have read in these pages can change your destiny also. I believe that God is reaching out to you through these words. He says, "Come to me all of you who are bowed down with sin and sorrow; come to me all of you who are weary and fed-up with stress. Come under My care, and learn of Me, and I will give you rest, and I will give you hope, and I will give you peace."

This book, could change your destiny!

Come with me on a journey, if you will, and I will take you to the beginning of time, no, even further back than that. I will show you a mystery that will both amaze and even scare you. But if you will dare to take my hand, and fly away for but a moment in time, I will open up a secret to you. And from a high distance I will show you something that is quite wonderful, and beyond all comprehension. I told you that I might even scare you, but be bold, and come on in, it's an adventure, and who knows? - you might even be glad that you came!

A man came to me one day and asked a rather difficult question. He said, "If God is all wise, and God is all knowing, and if God knows the future and all that is going to happen in it; and if God knew when he created the world that the first man he would ever make would mess the whole deal up by rebelling against Him, then why did He still make Him?" I said, "That's a good question! I do not know!"

So I went to God and asked Him. I reiterated the question to Him and said, "That's a good question, God. I mean, if You knew that

Adam would sin and turn away from you, and consequently bring chaos, and violence, and sickness, and death upon everything that You had so beautifully made, why on earth did you bother to create him?"

If I was God, and knew that all this trouble would come through one man's disobedience, I would never have formed him in the first place.

Supposing as God, I had decided not to look at the future, but just went ahead and fashioned man simply because I chose to do so, and then discovered the thing that I had created went bad, I would screw that Adam all up and throw him away. I would then create me a nice Adam who would never disobey me or fail me. I would create a man who would forever love and worship me.

So, as I was just sort of talking this thing

through with God, He began to show me an amazing truth that I had never known before.
He said, "Long before I ever made Adam, indeed long before I ever created the very first blade of grass that ever pushed its way through the finest soil that ever was found on this planet; and long before I designed and formed the first animal that ever breathed the purest air that ever filled the atmosphere, or the first fish that ever swam in the most crystal clear oceans; and long before I created the sun or the moon or the stars, and before I said those famous words, "Let there be light!",
I knew about you!
Even before I created the angels that serve before me continually, and before I flung the planets into space,
I saw you!

In the distant future, beyond the great mountains and hills that swelled up from beneath the heaving waters, and beyond the daybreaks of thousands of years and generations, I saw your face, I knew you then, and loved you, and must have you as My own. I wanted you to be My friend, and to inherit all that I own and possess.

And I knew that without Adam, even *that* Adam, you could never be. Unless it was him that I designed and brought into being, and breathed into his body the very breath of life, you would never exist, for without him you could not be born.

So, yes, I knew that this man would rebel and sin against me, and as a result bring upon himself and upon the whole world all sorts of misery and confusion and hurt.

So I put up with him, and watched as death,

hatred, violence, murder and innumerable other evils came upon this world through man's own wicked choices.

In fact the world became desperately violent at one stage, and the perversion and selfishness of the human race rose to heights that it had never been before. I decided I would rid Myself of this corruption, and destroy mankind from off the face of the earth.

I would send a great flood and wipe out every being that had life and breathed.

Then I remembered you!

So I saved just eight people alive in order that in time and generation you would still be born, even though it would be many thousands of years later.

And I put up with the provocation and disobedience of a created race that refused My ways and chose to do whatever it wanted.

I chose a nation called Israel to be My own special people, and I showed mighty signs and miracles among them. I delivered them time and time again from their enemies, but even then they utterly refused to let Me lead them or be their God.

Again and again I showed them My mercy and goodness and love, but they would not have Me, and rejected Me.

I sent to them My only Son, Jesus, and they spat on Him, and despised Him, and cursed Him, and as a final token to seal as it were their independence from Me, they beat Him and nailed His body to a cross.

And this they did publicly in the sight of all of heaven and all the angels.

But at that cross they never knew what they did, for this was also part of My own great plan to make a way for you to be My friend.

I saw you when you were first born in that little terraced house in Emmanuel Road, in Hastings, South East England. Quite an appropriate name for the street where you would begin your life! *[Emmanuel means 'God is with us']*

I saw you as you grew up. I watched over you through all the difficult times as well as the good times of your childhood. I saw the day when you would kneel in that flat in East London as a young man, and give your life to Me. That was so wonderful!"

WOW!!

And God sees you!

He knew you before the world began! He saw your face right back then.

He has seen every place that you have been. He never missed a thing.

He knew the person who would give you this book, and he knew the day you would actually pick it up and read it, - because He is God!

You may be in dire straits at this very moment; maybe your whole world is crumbling all around you. Pressures and difficulties, financial impossibilities, wrecked relationships, broken families, poor health - I don't know your particular situation, but let me recommend my Friend. His name is Jesus, and He has promised to anyone who is worn-out, under pressure, at the very point of giving up, to come to Him, to call on His name in faith, and He will rescue them and save them out of their troubles.

"Call on Me in the day of trouble, and I will deliver you, and you will give me thanks!"

He can deliver a miracle the very moment that you stand in the position of faith, trust, and confidence.

But how do I get this faith?

Well, actually, it is quite simple, and maybe that is what makes it so difficult for people to grasp!

Faith is a *gift* from God.

You can not have faith by *trying* to have faith!

To be precise, it comes by hearing. As you have read this book, so you have heard truths about God. The Bible says that faith comes by hearing, and hearing comes by the word of God. (That is why you should read the Bible).

If somehow God has spoken to you through these pages, then faith will have begun to rise in your heart.

I can not make anyone believe in God, or believe the truth about Jesus. I am just like the moon that hangs there in the darkness. I have no light or power or life of my own, but all that I can do is reflect (in some very small way) the truth of God's love to this degenerate world.

God is the light, and only He can shine into your darkness and bring life, and joy, and hope, and peace.

Jesus said, "I am the light of this world; if any one follows Me, they shall not walk in darkness, but have the light of life!"

The greatest miracle that could happen to you

right now is that you believe with all of your heart in Jesus Christ. And to do that you must do three things. You must firstly believe that He is the true Son of God, that He died for you on the cross in order that you might be forgiven and washed from all of your sin by His blood.

Secondly, you must be willing to repent. That is an old fashioned word, but so relevant today. What it simply means is that you must 'about-turn'. Turn from the direction that you are going in, and turn to God. Turn from what you know is wrong or evil, or sinful, and face Jesus Christ as the only one who can save you.

And thirdly, you must receive this Jesus into your heart and accept His *free* gift of salvation. The Bible says that whoever receives Jesus Christ and accepts Him as their only Saviour becomes a child of God, immediately! You cannot earn this or buy it. God's forgiveness, love, and salvation, is totally free to whoever will receive it!

To receive Jesus into your life you could pray this simple prayer:

Oh God, I acknowledge that I am a sinner. Please forgive my sin. Wash me with the blood that Jesus shed at the cross, and make me clean. I believe on Jesus with all my heart and ask Him to come into my life right now. Fill me with Your Holy Spirit, and make me Your child. I ask it in the name of Your holy Son Jesus, Amen.

Better still, tell Him the truth of where you are, of what you have been, and that you need Him right now to become your friend and Master (we call Him Lord). Talk to Him as the

One who knows everything there is to know about you. He has watched you since the day that you were born.

And now, if you have prayed that prayer, you should tell somebody. Don't keep it to yourself! God says that if you believe, you will not be ashamed to confess your personal faith in Jesus Christ. Get a Bible and begin to read the New Testament, and pray - it is not hard! Just talk to God as though He were your greatest friend - He is!

And it is so important to go to church or meet with other Christians *who believe the same things about God and the Bible as are written in this book.* There is an address at the back for you to write to, or a telephone number to call, or just go along.

There is nothing too hard for God!

No, your life and circumstances are not too difficult for Him!

Whatever your need, however desperate your situation, God can perform a miracle for you the moment that you dare to step out and trust Him with all of your heart.

I have proved Him again and again. He has never failed me.

Why don't you just say, "Yes" to Him, and receive Him right now?

This book comes with the compliments of: